iNDiA
THE LAND

Bobbie Kalman

A Bobbie Kalman Book

The Lands, Peoples, and Cultures Series

 Crabtree Publishing Company

The Lands, Peoples, and Cultures Series

Created by Bobbie Kalman

For the Karsons
Martha, Al, Cessa, and Miranda

Author: Bobbie Kalman

Third edition: Q2A

Editor: Sujatha Menon

Copy editor: Adrianna Morganelli

Proofreader: Crystal Sikkens

Editorial director: Kathy Middleton

Production coordinator: Katherine Berti

Prepress technician: Katherine Berti

Project manager: Santosh Vasudevan

Art director: Rahul Dhiman

First and second editions

> **Editors:** Jane Lewis, Christine Arthurs,
> Margaret Hoogeveen
> **Coordinating editor:** Ellen Rodger
> **Contributing editor:** Lisa Gurusinghe
> **Production coordinator:** Rose Gowsell

Cover: Dal Lake, in Jammu and Kashmir, is famous for its beautiful scenery and Victorian-era wooden houseboats.

Title page: The Ganges River flows through the ancient city of Varanasi, the holiest city in India.

Back cover: The elephant has been an important part of India's culture and history for centuries.

Illustrations:
Diane Eastman: icons
David Wysotski, Allure Illustrations: back cover

Map:
Jim Chernishenko

Photographs:
BigStockPhoto: Styve Reineck: p. 29
Courtesy of India tourist Organization: p. 19
Dennis Cox: p. 10, 24 (right), 25 (bottom)
Dinodia Images: Rajesh Vora: p. 21
Dreamstime: David Watts Jr.: p. 26
Ken Faris: p. 18
First Light: Jeremy Ferguson: p. 22
Four by Five: p. 6; Shostal: p. 14
Jacquie Gilbey/Ken Hood: p. 31 (bottom)
Catriona Gordon: p. 11 (bottom)
The Hindu: Nissar ahmad: p. 12; G Karthikeyan:
    p. 16; Ramesh kurup: p. 23 (top)
Istockphoto: Bob Thomas: p. 15
Wolfgang Kaehler: p. 24 (left)
Sudha and Abdullah Khandwani: p. 11 (top)
Jane Lewis: p. 1, 3
Eric Melis: p. 8
Photo Library: Guiziou Franck: p. 27 (bottom);
    Luca Invernizzi Tettoni: p. 30; Seux Paule/
    Hemis: front cover
Photo Researchers: Jefkin/Elkenave Photography:
    p. 25 (top); Charles D. Winters: p. 27 (top)
Ron Schroeder: p. 31 (top)
Shutterstock: p. 28; Galyna Andrushko: p. 4 (bottom);
    PhotoBarmaley: p. 4 (top); Ronald Sumners: p. 7
Mike Silver: p. 9, 20

Every effort has been made to obtain the appropriate credit and full copyright clearance for all images in this book. Any oversights, despite Crabtree's greatest precautions, will be corrected in future editions.

Library and Archives Canada Cataloguing in Publication

Kalman, Bobbie, 1947-
    India : the land / Bobbie Kalman. -- Rev. ed.

(The lands, peoples, and cultures series)
Includes index.
ISBN 978-0-7787-9285-7 (bound).--ISBN 978-0-7787-9655-8 (pbk.)

    1. India--Description and travel--Juvenile literature.
I. Title. II. Series: Lands, peoples, and cultures series

DS414.2.K34 2010   j954   C2009-901938-8

Library of Congress Cataloging-in-Publication Data

Kalman, Bobbie.
    India. The land / Bobbie Kalman. -- Rev. ed.
        p. cm. -- (The lands, peoples, and cultures series)
    Includes index.
    ISBN 978-0-7787-9655-8 (pbk. : alk. paper) -- ISBN 978-0-7787-9285-7
(reinforced library binding : alk. paper)
    1. India--Description and travel--Juvenile literature. I. Title. II. Series.

DS414.2.K34 2010
954--dc21

                                                2009013427

Crabtree Publishing Company

www.crabtreebooks.com   1-800-387-7650

Published in Canada
Crabtree Publishing
616 Welland Ave.
St. Catharines, ON
L2M 5V6

Published in the United States
Crabtree Publishing
PMB16A
350 Fifth Ave., Suite 3308
New York, NY 10118

Published in the United Kingdom
Crabtree Publishing
White Cross Mills
High Town, Lancaster
LA1 4XS

Published in Australia
Crabtree Publishing
386 Mt. Alexander Rd.
Ascot Vale (Melbourne)
VIC 3032

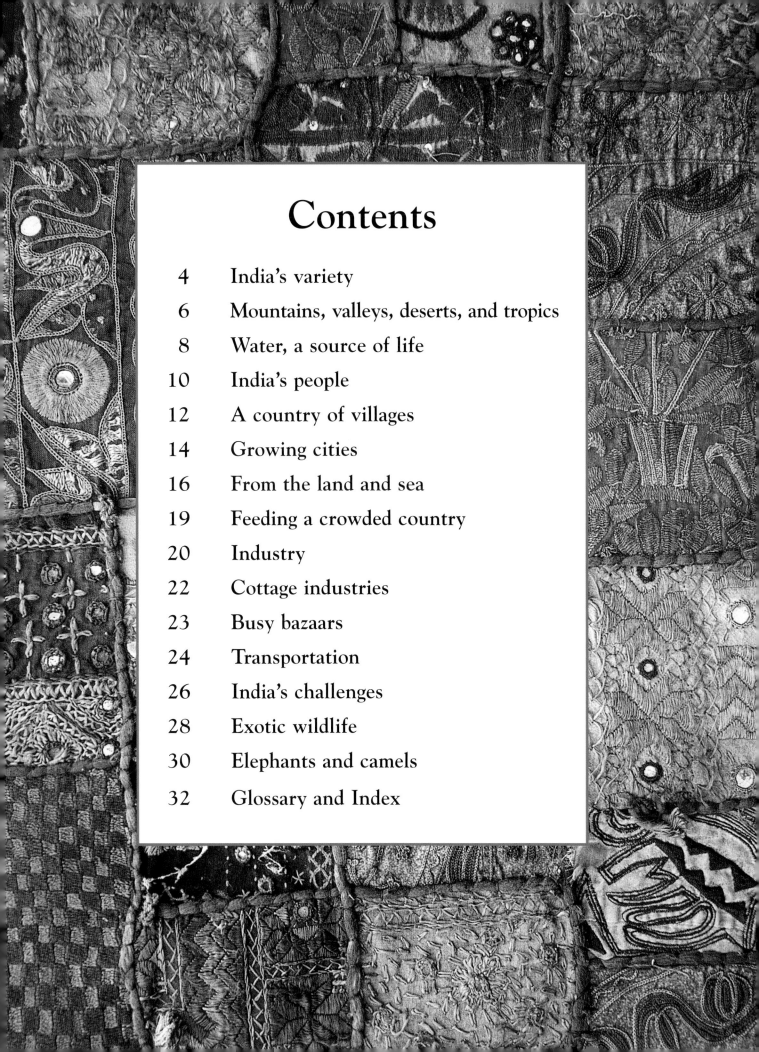

Contents

India's variety

India is a land of great variety. Within its borders snowy mountain peaks tower over lush green valleys; **fertile** plains contrast with treeless deserts. Mighty rivers and **tropical** rainforests add to the fascinating landscape. All this variety exists in India because it is a huge country. With 1,269,340 square miles (3,287,590 square kilometers), it is the seventh-largest country in the world. India is a country of contrasts. The past of this ancient land seems to exist alongside its present. Small villages with dirt roads can be found a short distance from huge, modern cities with wide, paved streets. **Artisans** skilled in ancient crafts live side by side with professionals who use the latest technology. Jets fly high above camel **caravans** slowly making their way across the Thar Desert.

The warm tropical areas of southern India contrast with the mountainous regions in the north.

India is located on the southern edge of the continent of Asia. A major portion of the country is a huge peninsula. A peninsula is a piece of land that is attached to the mainland but extends into a body of water. This part of India has the shape of an upside-down triangle jutting into the Indian Ocean. Off India's west coast is the Arabian Sea; off the east coast is the Bay of Bengal. India's neighbors are Pakistan, China, Tibet, Nepal, Bhutan, Myanmar (Burma), and Bangladesh. Just off India's southern tip is the small island nation of Sri Lanka. India itself is divided into 28 states and seven union territories.

Disputed borders

India and some of its neighbors disagree about exactly where their borders lie. India has border disputes with Bangladesh, China, and Pakistan. The India/Pakistan dispute is the most well known, and the most violent. Pakistan became a separate country after India gained independence from Britain in 1947. India and Pakistan disagreed about which country would claim the area of Jammu and Kashmir in the north. The countries have fought two major wars over the claim, and in recent years have come close to a third. The issue remains unresolved.

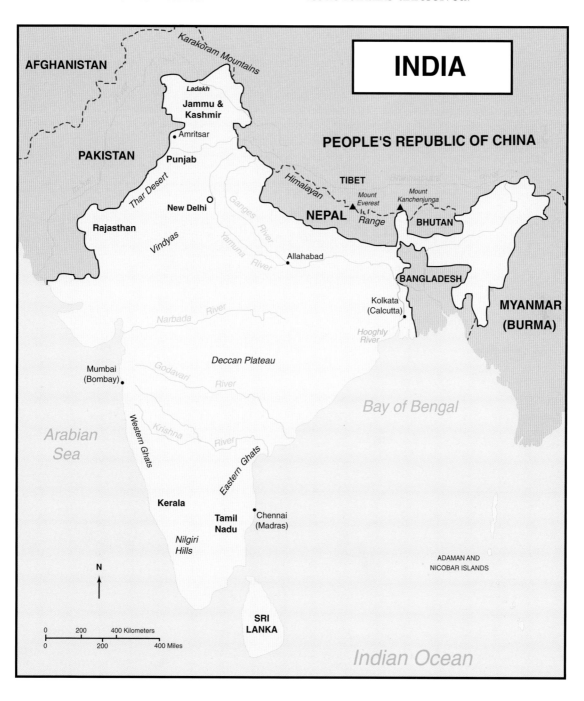

Mountains, valleys, deserts, and tropics

Across the northern part of India are the world's highest mountains, the Himalaya. This mountain range serves as a natural border between India and its neighbors. Some scientists believe that the lower part of India used to be an island. Over millions of years this island moved toward, and crashed into Asia. The collision caused the earth to buckle where the two land masses met, forcing up a ridge of towering mountains.

The Himalaya are not only the tallest, they are also the youngest mountains in the world. They are higher and steeper than older, weather-worn mountain ranges. Because the earth continues to shift, the Himalaya still grow a few centimeters each year, although wind and rain wear them down as fast as they grow.

(above) A camel and its owner take a rest before traveling on. Camels are well-suited for traveling in the desert regions of India.

In the ancient Indian Sanskrit language the word *himalaya* means "home of snow." The Himalayan mountains, averaging 20,000 feet (6,100 meters), are covered with snow all year round. Kanchenjunga, the tallest mountain in India, is part of the Himalayan range. At 28,209 feet (8,598 meters) it is only 984 feet (300 meters) shorter than Mount Everest, which is on the border of Nepal and Tibet. As you move south, the Himalaya become smaller.

A range of ranges

The Himalaya, together with several other ranges, make up one-sixth of India's land area. The Karakoram Mountains are located just west of the Himalaya, and the Vindyas separate the peninsula from northern India. Along the sides of the peninsula are the Western and Eastern Ghats. *Ghat* means "step." In a country with mountains as high as the Himalaya, you can see why smaller mountains might be called "steps."

Pale mists, bright flowers

The Nilgiri Hills are found at the southern tip of India, where the Western and Eastern Ghats meet. These rounded slopes are known as the Blue Hills because they are often covered in blue mist. Where there are mountains, there must be valleys, and India has some of the most beautiful valleys in the world. In summer the Vale of Kashmir in the foothills of the Himalaya is covered with a blanket of bright orange and yellow sunflowers. **Muslim** rulers once used this spot as a summer holiday destination.

Bone dry and baking hot

Two huge areas, the Deccan Plateau and the Thar Desert, are the hottest and driest areas of India. The Deccan Plateau, which covers most of the Indian peninsula, is barren with the exception of an occasional tuft of grass or scrub. The sun bakes the plateau, and temperatures rise as high as 113°F (45°C). The Thar Desert is located in northwestern India. It only receives about two inches (five centimeters) of rain a year, and sometimes none at all.

(below) Horses roam in a valley between the Himalayan mountains in Kashmir.

The heartland of India

The Indo-Gangetic Plain is the largest plain in the world. It is sometimes called the heartland of India because it is a highly productive agricultural region. For thousands of years water from melting snow has been flowing down from the Himalaya. As it travels across the land on its way to the sea, it leaves behind rich **deposits** and makes the land fertile. Three great rivers, the Brahmaputra, the Indus, and the Ganges, continue to **fertilize** the flat countryside as they flow through the plains.

A tropical climate

India has a tropical **climate**. Tropical climates are characterized by hot temperatures, dry winters, and wet summers. Spring is the hottest time of year. It is dry and dusty, and everyone feels tired and worn out. In June the wet season arrives. The rain comes down in buckets, and the farmers are pleased. The cool, dry winter begins in October. Nights can be chilly. Even though this general description applies to almost all of India, the climate varies from region to region. For instance, in Kerala the jungle remains lush even in the dry winter season. At the same time of year people in the north can go skiing!

Water, a source of life

Water is an important source of life. It is especially precious in India because water supplies often run low. During the dry season much of the country suffers from scorching heat and lack of water. Rivers become mere trickles, plants shrivel up, and many people go hungry because crops cannot grow.

The rainy season
In June the arrival of the monsoon season brings relief. A monsoon is a wind that picks up great amounts of water as it blows across the ocean. The water creates heavy, purple clouds that eventually burst. Rain comes pouring down in endless torrents, bringing the dusty earth back to life. The monsoon lasts until October.

Many areas rely entirely on the monsoon rains to provide moisture for their crops. Sometimes the monsoon enables farmers to grow a second crop so there will be enough food to last throughout the dry season. The rains can be a mixed blessing, however. Hard-hit communities suffer from severe flooding, which causes soil **erosion**, traffic accidents, drownings, and damage to homes and property.

Water management
Every year India must face the challenge of the never-ending cycle of wet and dry seasons. To manage their precious water supply, Indians build dams and **reservoirs** to store rainwater for future use. **Irrigation** systems channel water to farmers' fields. Rivers, reservoirs, and wells provide the water for the irrigation canals. Well water comes from groundwater, which is water that is absorbed by the earth when it rains.

Misusing well water
Recently, many wells have been dug in India. Some deep wells use up valuable groundwater, robbing the land of the moisture needed to keep it fertile. Plant and tree roots in the surrounding areas have difficulty reaching moisture. As a result, vegetation dies, and the land turns into desert. The misuse of well water has become a big problem. Large **plantations** use more than their fair share of water, so small farmers cannot get enough to grow their crops.

(below) Pilgrims travel to the city of Varanasi to bathe in the sacred water of the Ganges River.

Mighty rivers

The Ganges, the Brahmaputra, and the Indus rivers are all fed by melting glaciers in the Himalaya. India gets its name from the Indus River because Indian **civilization** began in the Indus Valley. Today the Indus flows mainly through Pakistan, but it also winds through northern India. Like the Indus River, the Brahmaputra only flows through a small part of India. At 1,802 miles (2,900 kilometers) it is one of the longest rivers in the world.

The Ganges River, also called the Ganga, is 1,557 miles (2,506 kilometers) long. It runs eastward through mountain valleys and across the fertile Indo-Gangetic Plain. The land along its banks is the most crowded area in the world. The Ganges eventually combines with the Brahmaputra and becomes the Padma River, which empties into the Bay of Bengal in Bangladesh. The Ganges and Padma rivers remain mighty even in the dry season and often burst their banks in the wet season.

From trickles to torrents

There are many other rivers in India, such as the Tapti, Narbada, Gadavari, and Krishna. These rain-fed rivers shrink in the dry season because there is not enough rain or melting snow at their sources to feed them all year round. During the rainy season they are transformed from trickles into gushing torrents. Many of India's powerful rivers have been dammed and are used to generate **hydroelectric** power.

Holy rivers

Water is so precious in India that rivers are considered sacred. For instance, the name Brahmaputra means "son of Brahma," the **Hindu** creator god. The Ganges is the most holy river of all. According to Hindu legend, the Ganges River once flowed through heaven. Many people make **pilgrimages** to visit holy places along this river.

(above) Every year during the rainy season India must cope with the problems caused by too much water.

India's people

India is a densely populated country. With more than one billion people, it has the second-largest population in the world. Only China has more people. India is smaller than China, and more crowded. Approximately 880 people live in each square mile (2.59 square kilometers) of India. This calculation is called the average population density.

Indigenous peoples

The first inhabitants of India were tribal people known as Adivasis. Today the Adivasis make up about eight percent of the total population. Their languages and customs are different from those of other Indians. Most Adivasis live in small self-contained communities scattered throughout the country. Many of these people have lost their land to development projects such as mines or hydroelectric dams. If the Adivasis lose their traditional land and homes, their way of life may disappear forever.

Ancient ancestors

Indian civilization is one of the oldest in the world. Some historians believe it is at least 10,000 years old. This ancient civilization began in the region of the Indus Valley (see map on page 5). About 3,000 or 4,000 years ago, the population began to move across northern India, as well as into the south.

Foreign influences

Muslim invaders arrived in the eleventh and sixteenth centuries, each time taking control of northern India. Over time, the Indian and Muslim **cultures** blended together in many ways. In the past 500 years, the Portuguese, British, French, and Dutch have also influenced India's people and culture.

The many faces of India

The long and complicated history of the Indian people resulted in the rich and varied culture of present-day India. Although Hindi is considered the main language, about 15 other official languages and hundreds of **dialects** are spoken throughout the country. Indians have different customs, practice a number of religions, and celebrate a variety of festivals.

Despite all these differences, Indians are held together by many common threads. About 80 percent of the population follows the Hindu religion. Only 14 percent of the population is Muslim, but the Muslim influence is strong. India's people also share a common history and strong sense of national pride.

(right) This girl lives in the desert region of Rajasthan. She is wearing traditional, colorful Rajasthani clothing.

(below) Namaste! *These Ladakhi children say hello in the Indian way.*

(opposite) India's population is growing quickly. By the middle of the twenty-first century India may have the largest population in the world.

A country of villages

Across the vast expanse of India there are more than half a million villages. Most of them have fewer than 1000 inhabitants each, yet in total, about 70 percent of the country's population live in these rural settlements. Every village is a unique community. Some are coastal fishing villages; others are farming towns.

Community living

An Indian village is a close-knit community. The homes are usually clustered together around a village square. From here the farmers walk to their fields every day and the fishermen head out to catch fish in nearby waters. Most village families have lived in the same village for countless **generations**. Each generation passes on the family's skills, knowledge, and land to its children. Most villagers live off the land, but in larger villages artisans such as weavers, potters, shopkeepers, and smiths provide services necessary for the well-being of the community. Farmers sell their produce, and vendors sell their wares at busy open-air markets called bazaars.

Changing village lifestyle

For centuries, time seemed to stand still in the rural villages. Each community took care of its own needs and rarely had contact with outsiders. Although much has stayed the same, villagers are now experiencing many changes. Today residents can travel quite easily from village to village using buses, cars, bicycles, and scooters.

Most villages have electricity, and many villagers have telephones, televisions, computers, and many other modern conveniences.

Covered wells

In the past, people had to carry water from faraway rivers or depend on open wells in the community. Open wells were a source of disease because bacteria thrived in them. To prevent disease, the government started a program to provide every village with a covered well. A covered well consists of a long tube sunk deep in the ground through which water can be pumped. Today, many of India's villages have covered wells powered by electric or hand-operated pumps.

A long way to go

Although some aspects of village life are improving, communities still face serious problems. Adequate sewage- and garbage-disposal systems do not exist in most villages. This is unhealthy for people and the environment. The land and water surrounding villages are contaminated with chemicals used in farming and with waste produced by a growing population. Many rural Indians do not have access to clean drinking water.

(above) Villagers harvest rice for food.

(opposite) Villagers go to the market or bazaar to buy food, conduct business, and catch up on the latest news.

Growing cities

Bursting at the seams

Some of India's cities have been around for hundreds of years; others are relatively new. In older cities, palaces, temples, and ancient city walls still stand as reminders of India's past. In the new sections, modern buildings create a different skyline. Whether old or new, all of India's cities share a common characteristic— they are growing at an incredibly fast rate. As a result, Indian cities have become overcrowded, and millions of people have nowhere to live.

India's capital

The capital city of India is New Delhi. It is located on the banks of the Yamuna River, a **tributary** of the Ganges. New Delhi has only been the capital of India since 1931. It is made up of two cities— a modern city that is less than 100 years old and a walled city, sometimes called Old Delhi, that has existed for centuries. Old Delhi was the home of the **Mogul** emperors. At that time it was known as Shahjahanabad, named after Shah Jahan, the ruler who had the city built.

(opposite) Mumbai is the nation's trading capital. This city is known as "The Gateway to India."

(below) New Delhi, the capital of India, has wide, modern streets.

The gateway to India

Mumbai, a city on the Arabian Sea, was built on the islands surrounding a natural harbor. In the past, traders came in sailing ships from distant lands. At that time, the city was called Bombay. All trading vessels anchored in the harbor before moving on to find India's spices and teas. Today Mumbai is a major center of foreign trade, finance, industry, and entertainment. With over 15 million people, Mumbai has the largest population of any Indian city.

Kolkata

Previously called Calcutta, Kolkata is located on the Hooghly River, which empties into the Bay of Bengal. Named after the Hindu goddess Kali, Kolkata was the capital city when India was a British colony. British-styled monuments and buildings are a common sight in the older section of the city. Today Kolkata is a major center of business, arts, and culture. It is the only Indian city with an underground subway.

Sacred city on the Ganges

Perhaps the city that best captures the spirit of India is Varanasi. Varanasi, located on the Ganges River, is both ancient and holy. Hindu pilgrims from all over India travel there to worship in temples and bathe in the sacred river. Varanasi may be the oldest living city on Earth.

(above) At the end of the day giant fishing nets are hung out to dry over the sparkling sea.

A shortage of land

Many farmers cannot make an adequate living because of a shortage of land. After generations of dividing up the land among children, farmers are left with tiny farms. As a result, some farmers are being forced to sell their farmland to large landowners. Others rent land from landowners who take up to one half of the harvest for themselves and leave very little for the farmers. This practice is called **sharecropping**. One of the major causes of poverty in India is that farmland is not distributed fairly. Consequently, thousands of landless farmers move to the cities each year in search of work.

Fishing

The seas surrounding India are valuable **natural resources**. Coastal fishing has become a profitable industry. Mackerel, sardines, shark, perch, sole, prawn, and tuna are caught in the sea. Part of the catch is transported in refrigerated train compartments to markets across the country. The rest is frozen and exported to other countries. Shrimp is the most popular export. Frog legs, lobster tails, and shark fins are other Indian delicacies enjoyed by people around the world. Freshwater fishing is also done. Indians catch carp and catfish from inland rivers.

From the land and sea

Two-thirds of India's people make their living from the land. With a rapidly growing population, the country's farmers must work hard to feed all the citizens. This can be a challenging task because many parts of India are too dry to support crops.

The most fertile farming areas are the Indo-Gangetic Plain, the eastern river **delta** by the Bay of Bengal, the Punjab, and the coastlines. India is the second largest producer of rice in the world, after China. Rice is grown in most regions of India. In drier areas such as the Deccan Plateau and the Punjab, wheat is the most important crop. Peanuts, green peas, cotton, and tobacco are also grown there. In the northern mountain regions, barley, potatoes, apples, peaches, cherries, walnuts, and tea are grown. In India's lush tropical regions all sorts of foods are grown, such as coconuts, jackfruit, mangoes, bananas, citrus fruits, pineapple, papaya, cashew nuts, sugar cane, and ginger.

(below) Modern farming machinery and techniques have changed the agricultural practice in rural India.

Modern machines

Until recently all farming chores were done by hand with the help of water buffalo or oxen. Today tractors, threshing machines, and other types of modern equipment ease the workload on large farms. Most family farms, however, still use traditional tools and methods of farming. Many small farmers cannot afford modern equipment or the tools and parts required to fix machines when they break down. They also lack the special skills needed to operate and repair the machines. Changing from traditional methods of farming to new techniques takes a great deal of money, time, and training.

Farming problems

Indian farmers must cope with many serious problems. Their crops depend on an unpredictable supply of water. If there is a flood or a drought, crops fail. A drought is a long period of time when there is no rain. Dry regions must rely on wells, reservoirs, and irrigation systems for their water supply. Modern wells are powered by electricity, which is often in short supply.

One of India's greatest challenges is to provide adequate food for its ever-growing population. Prior to the 1960s India had to buy large amounts of food from other countries because its own farms could not produce enough to feed the entire population.

The Green Revolution

In the 1960s India experienced the Green Revolution. The Green Revolution was an enormous increase in farming production. New wells and irrigation projects, modern farming machinery, chemical fertilizers, and pesticides all made this agricultural growth possible. Scientists from Japan and Mexico developed a new type of hardy wheat grain that could produce four times the amount that ordinary wheat could produce. Indian farmers began to plant this new grain and, in less than ten years, the amount of wheat they grew doubled. The Green Revolution helped make India **self-sufficient** in food production.

(opposite) In the past 40 years India has been producing more abundant crops than ever before.

Cash instead of food?

Farmers who grow cash crops have benefited enormously from the Green Revolution. Cash crops are grown in large quantities on huge plantations and then exported to other countries. Sugar cane, grown in the central regions of India, is a cash crop. It is refined and sold as packaged sugar. Tea is another example. India is famous around the world for its flavorful teas. Other cash crops include rubber, tobacco, cotton, and coffee. Although cash crops may be profitable for some, they take up land that could otherwise grow the grains, fruits, and vegetables necessary to provide a hungry nation with a balanced diet.

Some cash-crop farmers are using up too much groundwater, so the land is in danger of becoming a desert. Other plantations abuse the land while trying to produce as much as possible as quickly as possible. They plant one crop right after harvesting another crop, so the soil is unable to replace its **nutrients**.

(above) Tea is a cash crop. Pickers, such as this woman, work on tea plantations in the Nilgiri Hills and the hilly areas of northeast India.

Industry

India is considered one of the world's most **industrialized** nations. Indian companies make everything from computers to chocolate bars. Many industries are owned by the government, but more and more privately owned companies are being established in India.

Natural resources

One of the reasons that India has so much industry is that the country is rich in a variety of natural resources such as coal, iron ore, natural gas, copper ore, and oil. Most of India's manufacturing is based on these natural resources. Coal and oil industries provide energy for homes as well as factories. Other energy sources are hydroelectric dams and nuclear power plants. The Steel Authority of

(above) Indian textile-making has developed into an art.

India produces steel from iron, which is used to build machines, cars, tools, and many other products. Rubber is another natural resource that is plentiful in India. It comes from a special tree and is used to make tires, rubber boots, and all kinds of other useful products.

Self-sufficiency

When India first became an independent nation, it had to import most of its manufactured goods. Today India makes its own bicycles, tractors, trucks, railway cars, scooters, and ships. It also manufactures electronics, plastics, chemicals, computers, and computer software. To build up industry, the government encourages joint ventures. Joint ventures are businesses that are owned by both Indian and foreign investors. An example of a joint venture in India is the Maruti car company, which is owned by Japanese people and Indians.

The ancient textile industry

Centuries ago Indians developed weaving skills and styles that have become world famous. Cloth was woven on hand looms by a special group of artisans. Dyeing was done by another. The skills of weaving and dyeing were passed on from generation to generation.

Today the textile industry is the backbone of Indian manufacturing. India has become the third-largest cotton producer in the world. It also produces great quantities of silk, wool, and jute. Most materials are woven on machines in huge factories. Cotton fabric and other textiles are made into shirts, pants, and dresses, which are then exported, or the material itself is shipped to clothing factories in other countries.

(above) Handpainted posters advertise the latest hit movies.

Movies galore

India's film-making industry is the largest in the world, releasing hundreds of movies a year. Mumbai (previously called Bombay) is the major center of movie making—the industry in that city is nicknamed "Bollywood." Most Bollywood movies are musical romances with a lot of singing and dancing. Movies are also made in Chennai and Kolkata. Films produced in those cities tend to be more artistic or serious, covering social conditions and problems.

Pollution

Due to the huge amount of industry in India, pollution has become a major problem. Coal-burning factories spew out dangerous fumes, covering the cities with blankets of smog. Few pollution controls exist to cope with the wastes. Toxic waste is frequently dumped into the air and water and onto the land, with little concern for the environment. Many cities still do not have adequate waste-disposal systems to cope with their garbage and sewage.

India has a tradition of producing beautiful and useful products in its cottage industries. Cottage industries are businesses that are conducted in people's homes. Most of these industries are based on ancient skills and techniques passed down through the generations. Spinning, weaving, and the creation of carpets, toys, wickerware, and pottery are just some examples of cottage industries. Today many cottage-industry products are sold in Indian cities and to other countries.

Handmade beauty

Mahatma Gandhi was a national leader who led India's struggle for independence. He strongly urged Indians to maintain their traditional village crafts. He believed that developing these crafts would help villages become self-sufficient and make India strong. Today the government continues to encourage cottage industries because they provide jobs for villagers. Some village artisans are going out of business because there is not enough demand for their goods. Their wares cost more money than inexpensive, factory-made goods. The handmade products of skilled artisans, however, are still prized for their quality and unmatched beauty.

(below) Instead of having a door and windows, this shoemaker's shop is open to the street.

Busy bazaars

Markets, called bazaars, are part of every Indian city and large village. Bazaars are busy streets and lanes where items are bought and sold.

Each street is lined with many tiny shops. Merchants also sell their goods from stalls, carts, and mats spread out on the ground.

Every imaginable kind of item can be found at an Indian bazaar. Fresh vegetables, lime juice, glittering gold and silver jewelry, garlands of marigolds, sticky sweets, clothes, and books are all for sale. Street stalls also offer a variety of services. You can get your hair cut, a letter typed, your fortune told, your ears cleaned, a tooth filled, or have a bite to eat.

Who's the better bargainer?

If you shop at an Indian bazaar, you must know how to bargain. When you ask the price of an item, the vendor tells you how much he or she wants for it. The cost, however, is not fixed. You are expected to say how much you are willing to pay. After some discussion, you and the vendor agree on a price, and a deal is made.

(left and below) Indian bazaars display varied interesting items for sale. Most of the time they are bustling with people.

Looking at a busy city street in India for the first time, you might wonder how people manage to reach their destinations. Cars, trucks, buses, taxis, bicycles, motorcycles, and pedestrians all compete for road space. You might see four people on a scooter bolting into traffic or a bicycle **rickshaw** squeezing its way between two moving trucks. The confusing flow of vehicles can become more congested due to slow-moving **bullock** carts and wandering cows. In some areas you will even find camels, mules, and elephants on the streets.

Indian Airlines

One of the safest ways to travel in India is by air. The national airline, Indian Airlines, flies passengers, mail, and cargo throughout India. Altogether, India has more than 280 airports. Eight cities have international airports.

Rural travel

With 70 percent of the population living in rural villages, walking from place to place is still a main means of transportation. Riding in a bullock cart is also a common way of traveling. Some bullock carts have wooden wheels, causing the passengers to have bumpy rides. Rubber tires make the ride more comfortable, but they are an expensive luxury that only some villagers can afford. Farmers who have tractors use them for more than just plowing fields. They drive them on the roads,

using them to transport both people and goods. To shield passengers from the hot sun, tractors are often equipped with umbrellas.

A far-reaching network

The Indian railway network is the fourth-longest in the world. There are 39,078 miles (62,915 kilometers) of track crisscrossing the country. Indian trains carry ten million passengers each day! Those who can afford the fare ride first class in compartments with cushioned chairs. Most people, however, travel second class. Second-class cars are cheaper, but they are always crowded. Bench seats are folded up into beds at night, so passengers sleep one above another in bunk bed style. Some passengers stand near the wide-open doors to breathe the fresh air and avoid the cramped quarters.

(above) Indians often decorate their vehicles. This auto-rickshaw is adorned with flower garlands and sparkling trim.

(left) City streets in India are packed with all kinds of vehicles.

Brimful buses

People prefer to take trains, but many also take buses. Buses are used for traveling between villages and for public transportation within cities. Buses are often jam-packed and stifling hot inside. They are so crowded with people, luggage, and livestock such as chickens and goats, that people sit on the floor, hang out the door, or ride on the roof! Not all buses are crowded and uncomfortable, however. Some "deluxe" buses are shiny, air-conditioned coaches that show video movies during the ride.

Rocky roads

In the past, Indian villages were almost impossible to reach because there were no roads. Today most places are connected by roads, but there are no major multi-lane highways. Many country roads, full of potholes and rocks, are better suited for bullock carts than modern vehicles. Roads and bridges are often washed out during the monsoon season. City streets are paved, but traffic is so congested that at times the roads are transformed into parking lots!

(above) Bullock carts can pull heavy loads and manage difficult roads.

(inset) Traveling by bus is so popular that passengers often have to ride on the roof.

India has one of the highest numbers of traffic mishaps in the world. Poor road and rail conditions, careless driving, and vehicles that are in need of repair are the causes of many accidents. Since buses and trains are often overcrowded, the number of deaths is high when accidents occur.

India's challenges

The new millennium brings new challenges to all the countries in the world. India has many issues to deal with in the twenty-first century. A rapidly growing population, environmental concerns, proper **sanitation**, clean drinking water, and energy production are a few of the most pressing problems in the country today.

Overflowing with people

The population of India is growing at a high rate. Every year it increases by almost two percent, or more than 20 million people a year! At this rate, India will soon have more people than any other country in the world, including China. It will be difficult for India to support this huge population. The country already has a hard time providing food, housing, education, health care, and jobs for all its citizens. Overpopulation is one of the greatest challenges India faces today.

Pollution problems

India's pollution problems are growing along with its population. Emissions from thousands of factories and millions of cars are a huge source of air pollution. New Delhi is one of the world's most polluted cities. Chemicals used by India's farmers are poisoning the ground and water. An increased use of plastic and disposable products is creating more and more garbage, and few cities have the ability to deal with so much waste. The Indian government and other organizations have only just begun to tackle this difficult issue.

Unhealthy conditions

Poor sanitation is the cause of many health problems in India. Two-thirds of the population do not have access to basic sanitation in the form of proper toilets and clean drinking water. Disease and infection spread quickly in unsanitary conditions. People get sick with **dysentery** and other illnesses because they drink unsafe water. Many regions are without public toilets, so human waste is left in the streets. During the monsoon season the air is hot and extremely humid. Disease-causing bacteria multiply and spread in these damp conditions. Today Indians receive better health care than ever before. Far fewer people die from **malaria**, **tuberculosis**, **leprosy**, or dysentery, but these diseases are still a serious problem in India.

Big dam projects

Since India gained independence from Britain in 1947, the country has built hundreds of dams. Rivers are dammed in order to provide hydro-electric power and to divert clean water for drinking and irrigation to villages. The negative effects of dams, however, are becoming known. Millions of people lose their land and homes due to flooding. Forests are destroyed, animals lose their habitats, and diseases such as malaria spread more rapidly. The soil around dams slowly degrades, which kills plants and crops. Dam projects cost a huge amount of money. India's challenge in the coming years is to decide whether this money could be better spent.

(above) These children are gathered around the neighborhood water pump. This is the only source of water for drinking, cooking, and bathing for the families that live nearby.

(below) Without proper disposal systems, garbage is often left on the street. Animals do their part to help clean up.

(opposite) India's growing population means more vehicles on the roads, more industry, and more pollution.

 # Exotic wildlife

Some of the most exotic animals in the world come from India. At one time they were abundant in their natural habitats all over the country. The Asian lion and the Indian gazelle roamed the grasslands, whereas the camel toured the desert. Forests were alive with the roar of the elephant and the chatter of the monkey. In the jungles the wild buffalo and the one-horned rhinoceros were once found. The snow leopard made its home in the Himalayan mountains. The panther, the cheetah, and the Royal Bengal tiger have lived in India for 70 million years. Magnificently colored exotic birds such as the peacock also added to the country's wildlife.

Just as animal **species** all over the world are disappearing, Indian wildlife is also dwindling rapidly. Over the centuries, as the population of India increased, more and more land was cleared and settled, leaving less and less room for animal habitats. Today most of the animal habitats have disappeared to make way for farms, cities, and massive projects such as hydroelectric dams.

Overhunting is another major cause of the loss of wildlife. India has a long tradition of hunting for sport. In the past, hunting expeditions took place on the estates of the Maharajahs, or Indian princes. Europeans flocked to India in pursuit of big game.

28

Protecting endangered species

Many of India's animals are now **endangered** species. Fewer than 250 Asian lions are left. The one-horned rhinoceros is also endangered, as are the Asian elephant, black panther, snow leopard, and tiger. To protect these and other animals, the government has set up hundreds of wildlife parks and reserves. Many old hunting grounds have been turned into national parks. Today there are strict hunting rules. Only a certain kind and number of animals can be killed every year on special animal reserves, and hunting endangered animals is illegal.

(below) Game reserves protect wildlife such as this Asian lion.

(opposite) The Royal Bengal tiger is India's national animal. Most tigers are orange and black, but these are rare white Bengal tigers.

Preying poachers

Despite all these protective measures poachers, or people who kill wild animals illegally, make huge amounts of money. Some people are willing to pay extremely high prices for luxurious fur coats and ivory carvings made from elephant tusks.

The majestic tiger

The Royal Bengal tiger is the national animal of India. This tiger is the largest member of the cat family and possesses striking stripes. Indian folklore is full of stories about the majestic ways of tigers. Yet people's high regard for the tiger has not protected it from being overhunted. In the 1970s fewer than 1000 of these animals remained in India. As a result, hunting the tiger became illegal, and tiger habitats were preserved. Although the tiger population has made a comeback, the species is still endangered.

Elephants and camels

Elephants that are native to India are smaller than African elephants. For centuries, Asian elephants have been trained to perform many useful tasks because they are strong and intelligent beasts. At one time they were ridden into battle by the Indian army. Today, they are used in the logging industry to pull trees and haul heavy logs.

Elephant school

Elephants begin training when they are five years old. Their trainers are called *mahouts*. At the beginning of training, a team of *mahouts* strokes the elephant over and over again until the animal gets used to the presence of people. It is bathed and scrubbed down every day as a reward for its hard work. By the end of the seven-year training period, an elephant can respond to up to 40 vocal commands. A *mahout* and his sensitive student often become lifelong companions.

Endangered elephants

The elephant has been an important part of India's culture and history. Unfortunately, these animals have lost much of their natural habitat to **deforestation** and agriculture. Some people still hunt elephants for their ivory tusks, even though it is illegal. The number of Asian elephants living in the wild is rapidly decreasing. Sadly, the species has now been declared endangered.

(above) Elephants are often painted and decorated before they appear in parades and festivals.

(opposite) Some camel owners shave their animals to create intricate raised designs. Others use colorful beads and blankets for decoration.

Long distance loads

Camels carry people and packages across the Thar Desert. Camel caravans wind their way through dry terrain and rocky hills, loaded down with goods and dressed in elaborate garb. Like a horse, a camel wears a saddle, reins, and stirrups. The bridle is clipped onto a camel's nostrils instead of being held in its mouth because the animal is constantly chewing its cud. A proud owner also drapes a fancy saddle blanket over the camel's back. The best decorations of all are the bells that tinkle softly in the desert wind.

Camel secrets

People have often wondered how camels can travel such long distances without taking a drink. They used to think that camels stored water inside their humps. Camels do not store water; they conserve it. The fat deposits in their humps are used as energy. Camels also have flexible body temperatures and sweat very little. When they do get a chance to drink, they can slurp up 26 gallons (100 liters) of water in less than ten minutes!

Camel capers

Camels are well known for their stubborn nature and nasty personalities. When they get upset, they spit, hiss, and bite. Although it is often difficult to get a camel to follow orders, cooperative ones can move quickly. The fastest camels have been clocked at speeds of over 40 miles (65 kilometers) per hour.

Glossary

artisan A skilled craftsperson

bullock A docile bull

caravan A group of people and pack animals on a journey

civilization A society with a well-established culture that has existed for a long period of time

climate The normal long-term weather conditions for an area

culture The customs, beliefs, and arts of a distinct group of people

deforestation The process of cutting down many trees in one area

delta A mass of sand, mud, and soil that settles at the mouth of a river

deposit A mass of material that builds up by a natural process

dialect A variation of a language

dysentery An infection of the intestine, which causes pain and severe diarrhea

endangered Very close to becoming extinct

erosion The gradual washing away of soil and rocks by rain, wind, or running water

fertile Able to grow many plants or crops

fertilize To add nutrients to soil to make it better for growing plants

generation People born at about the same time. Grandparents, parents, and children make up three generations

Hindu A follower of Hinduism—an ancient Indian religion based on the holy books called the *Vedas*

hydroelectricity Electricity produced by waterpower

industrialized A term used to describe a society that produces manufactured goods in factories

irrigation The process of bringing water to the land, usually farmers' fields, so that crops can grow

leprosy A disease that destroys the nerves, causing deformation and death

malaria A disease that is spread by mosquitoes

Mogul A Muslim empire that existed in India between the 1500s and 1800s

Muslim A follower of the Islamic religion

natural resource Anything that exists in nature and is useful to human beings. Forests, mineral deposits, and water are all natural resources

nutrient A substance that living things need in order to grow

pilgrimage A journey to a sacred place or shrine

plantation A huge farm that grows cash crops and employs many workers

reservoir A large, natural or human-made store of water

rickshaw A small, three-wheeled vehicle for one or two passengers

sacred Holy

sanitation Clean conditions for healthy living

self-sufficient Able to take care of oneself

sharecropping A type of farming whereby a portion of the harvest is given to a landowner as rent

species A distinct animal or plant group that shares similar characteristics and can produce offspring

tributary A river that flows into a larger river

tropical Describing a hot, humid climate

tuberculosis A deadly disease, caused by poor sanitation, that affects the lungs and bones

Index

Printed in China—CT